Rhythm of the Unseen

Unseen

*The Bizarre Dancing Plague of 16th-
Century Europe*

Brian Hughes

ISBN: 979-8-3975-4935-6

Cover designed by: Alexander Cole

Written-Right Publications

Printed in the United States of America

Table of Contents

Chapter One

The year was 1518, and the quaint city of Strasbourg, nestled along the banks of the Rhine River, witnessed a bewildering and unprecedented event. In the sweltering heat of summer, a woman named Frau Troffea stepped out onto the cobblestone streets and began to dance. Her movements were at first graceful and fluid, captivating the attention of passersby. However, as the hours turned into days, something far more extraordinary unfolded. Frau Troffea's solitary dance soon attracted other individuals, who joined her in the rhythm and fervor of their own inexplicable movements. The contagion spread like wildfire, engulfing the city in a sea of twirling bodies and exhausted souls. This bizarre episode, known as the Dancing Plague of 1518, would forever imprint itself in the annals of history and puzzle scholars and researchers for centuries to come.

To understand the true significance of the dancing plague, it is imperative to delve into the historical tapestry of 16th-century

Europe. The continent was undergoing profound transformations, both in its social fabric and intellectual landscapes. The Renaissance, with its celebration of humanism, scientific inquiry, and artistic creativity, was in full swing. However, the era was not without its darker undertones. Religious tensions simmered, culminating in the upheaval of the Protestant Reformation, which challenged the authority of the Catholic Church and fragmented the unity of the Christian faith. Against this backdrop of religious turmoil, political rivalries, and economic upheavals, the dancing plague emerged as a haunting enigma, a macabre spectacle that defied conventional explanations.

This book sets out on a multidisciplinary journey to unravel the mysteries of the Dancing Plague of 1518. By drawing upon historical accounts, medical records, sociological perspectives, and psychological insights, we aim to shed light on this perplexing phenomenon. Our goal is to provide a comprehensive examination of the outbreak, its causes, and its implications, situating it within the broader context of the time and exploring its enduring historical significance. Through meticulous research, analysis, and interpretation, we seek to deepen our understanding of collective behavior, the interplay of cultural and social factors, and the complexities of the human mind when confronted with the inexplicable.

This book is organized into fifteen chapters, each exploring a different facet of the Dancing Plague of 1518. Chapter 2 delves into the initial outbreak in Strasbourg, examining the first cases and the reactions they elicited. Chapter 3 offers a detailed account of the dance itself, exploring the physical manifestations and symptoms exhibited by the afflicted individuals. In Chapter 4, we investigate the spread of the plague beyond Strasbourg's borders, tracing its trajectory to neighboring towns and regions.

Chapter 5 delves into the medical and religious explanations offered at the time, shedding light on the prevailing theories and beliefs surrounding the phenomenon. Building upon this, Chapter 6 presents modern retrospective analyses and hypotheses, exploring various possible causes, from mass hysteria to ergotism and psychological factors. In Chapter 7, we delve into the social and cultural factors that may have contributed to the outbreak, examining the role of superstition, fear, and collective behavior in 16th-century Europe.

Chapter 8 explores the responses and interventions of local authorities, religious institutions, and medical practitioners in the face of this bewildering crisis. In Chapter 9, we examine the impact of the dancing plague on daily life, exploring its economic and social consequences, and the disruption it caused to normal activities and routines.

Chapter 10 focuses on the decline and eventual end of the dancing plague, unraveling the factors that contributed to the subsiding of the dancing craze. In Chapter 11, we delve into the historical significance and interpretations of the phenomenon, exploring its enduring legacy and the lessons learned from it as interpreted by historians and scholars.

Chapter 12 takes a comparative approach, examining similar instances of mass hysteria or collective behavior throughout history and contrasting them with the dancing plague. In Chapter 13, we shift our focus to psychological and sociological perspectives, analyzing the phenomenon through the lenses of psychology and sociology, and exploring its relevance to contemporary understandings of collective behavior.

Chapter 14 delves into the representation of the dancing plague in popular culture, exploring references to the phenomenon in literature, art, and media, and examining its influence on popular culture and artistic expressions. Finally, in Chapter 15, we conclude our exploration with a summary of key findings and insights gained throughout the book, offering final thoughts on the Dancing Plague of 1518.

By traversing this comprehensive and interdisciplinary journey, we aim to shed light on the enigmatic phenomenon that gripped Strasbourg centuries ago. Through meticulous research, analysis, and interpretation, we seek to deepen our understanding of the dancing plague's historical context, its causes, and its far-reaching implications. As we embark on this intellectual exploration, let us unravel the threads of history and delve into the captivating mystery of the Dancing Plague of 1518.

Chapter Two

In the summer of 1518, the picturesque city of Strasbourg bustled with its usual activities. The warm breeze carried the scent of freshly baked bread from the local bakeries, while merchants bartered goods in the bustling market squares. Yet, unbeknownst to the inhabitants, an invisible storm was brewing, a phenomenon that would soon shake the very foundations of their tranquil lives.

It was in the narrow alleyways of Strasbourg that the extraordinary began to unfold. One fateful day, a woman named Frau Troffea stepped onto the cobblestone streets and started dancing. Her movements were elegant, almost mesmerizing, drawing the attention of passersby. At first, it seemed like a harmless display of exuberance, a spontaneous burst of joy. However, as the hours passed, it became apparent that something was amiss. Frau Troffea continued to dance, heedless of exhaustion, her body seemingly driven by an invisible force.

As news of Frau Troffea's relentless dance spread throughout the city, a sense of unease gripped the inhabitants. Curiosity turned to concern, and concern soon morphed into fear. And yet, despite the growing apprehension, some individuals felt an inexplicable compulsion to join Frau Troffea in her trance-like movements. Like a peculiar magnetism, the dance lured them in, drawing them into its frenzied embrace.

Days turned into nights, and nights bled into days as the number of dancers multiplied. What began as a solitary dance now became a collective display of frenetic energy. The streets of Strasbourg pulsated with bodies twirling, spinning, and contorting in a hypnotic rhythm. The infected dancers formed a chaotic mosaic, their limbs intertwining, their faces etched with both ecstasy and agony.

The arrival of the dancing plague threw Strasbourg into disarray. The city's authorities, perplexed and alarmed, grappled with how to respond to this inexplicable phenomenon. Fear and uncertainty spread like wildfire, seeping into the very fabric of society. Some believed the dancing to be a divine punishment, while others saw it as a sign of impending doom. Amidst the chaos, daily life came to a grinding halt as the city became consumed by the dance.

Throughout the outbreak, many individuals documented their observations of the dancers. Physicians, priests, and concerned citizens alike sought to understand the nature of this affliction. Descriptions of the dancers varied, but there were commonalities. The afflicted exhibited a frenzied energy, their movements rapid and unrelenting. Their bodies, drenched in sweat, showed signs of exhaustion, yet they danced on, seemingly impervious to pain or fatigue.

As news of the dancing plague spread beyond the city walls, people from neighboring towns and regions looked on in disbelief. Speculations ran rampant, with various theories attempting to make sense of this bizarre phenomenon. Some attributed it to supernatural forces, while others blamed it on demonic possession. Physicians and scholars offered medical explanations, invoking imbalances of bodily humors or disturbances in the nervous system.

One of the most puzzling aspects of the dancing plague was its contagious nature. The sight of individuals caught in the grip of the dance seemed to trigger a chain reaction, drawing in others like moths to a flame. Witnesses reported how onlookers, initially mere spectators, became unwitting participants, unable to resist the compulsion to join the swirling mass of dancers. The contagious nature of the plague raised perplexing questions about the underlying mechanisms driving this collective behavior.

Faced with the escalating crisis, Strasbourg's authorities struggled to find effective measures to contain the outbreak. They initially attempted to quell the dancing by imposing restrictions and issuing orders to disperse the crowds. However, these measures proved futile, as the dancers seemed impervious to commands and driven solely by their unrelenting movements. The city's authorities found themselves grappling with an unprecedented situation that defied their understanding and conventional methods of control.

The dancing plague's emergence had profound social repercussions in Strasbourg. The fabric of the city's daily life was torn asunder, with routines and responsibilities abandoned in the face of the all-consuming dance. Workplaces were left empty, families were disrupted, and communal gatherings took on a surreal and frenzied atmosphere. The contagion of the dance permeated not only bodies but also the social structures and interactions of the city, leaving a lasting impact on its collective consciousness.

Amidst the chaos and spectacle, it is crucial not to overlook the individual experiences of the dancers themselves. For those caught in the grip of the dancing plague, the relentless movements became a personal torment. Accounts describe their expressions of pain and anguish mixed with moments of ecstatic abandon. Their bodies, pushed to the limits of endurance, bore the physical toll of the incessant dance, while their minds grappled with the torment of an inexplicable compulsion.

As the outbreak persisted, Strasbourg became a hub of speculation, attracting scholars, physicians, and religious figures seeking to unlock the mysteries of the dancing plague. The city's medical practitioners pondered the causes, drawing upon the prevailing medical theories of the time, including imbalances of bodily humors or astrological influences. Meanwhile, religious authorities pondered the plague's significance within a spiritual framework, searching for signs and omens from the divine.

As the days turned into weeks, and the dance continued unabated, desperation began to seep into the hearts of Strasbourg's inhabitants. The initial intrigue and curiosity evolved into fear and desperation for a solution. People sought remedies from traditional healers, turned to religious rituals, and even resorted to exorcisms in an attempt to free the afflicted from the dance's grip. Yet, the plague persisted, seemingly defying all attempts at intervention.

The outbreak's initial days marked the beginning of a perplexing chapter in Strasbourg's history. The dancing plague's sudden emergence, its contagious nature, and the relentless movements of the afflicted captivated the city and stirred the imagination of those beyond its borders. The outbreak raised profound questions about the limits of human understanding, the power of collective behavior, and the inherent mysteries of the human mind.

Chapter Three

The dance that consumed the afflicted individuals during the Dancing Plague of 1518 was unlike any other. It defied conventional notions of choreography and rhythm, weaving a tapestry of bizarre movements that captivated and confounded observers. In this chapter, we delve into the intricate details of the dance itself, seeking to unravel its enigmatic nature and explore the physical manifestations and symptoms exhibited by those caught in its relentless grip.

Witnesses described the dance as a frenzied display of movement, with limbs flailing and bodies contorting in seemingly unnatural ways. It was as if the dancers were possessed by an otherworldly energy that propelled them into a state of perpetual motion. The movements lacked grace and precision, defying traditional dance forms and existing outside the realm of structured choreography. Instead, the afflicted individuals seemed to be guided by an internal rhythm, an unseen force dictating their every twist and turn.

One of the defining characteristics of the dancing plague was the dancers' relentless motion. They danced for hours on end, without respite or reprieve. Their bodies seemed impervious to fatigue, driven by an inner compulsion that overrode physical limitations. However, as the dance persisted, exhaustion inevitably set in. Witnesses noted the gradual deterioration of the dancers' physical stamina, their movements becoming more labored and their bodies showing signs of weariness. Yet, the dance persisted, a testament to the mysterious power that held them in its grip.

The dance, paradoxically, evoked a range of emotions in the afflicted individuals. While some experienced moments of ecstatic abandon, their faces radiant with joy and liberation, others were consumed by torment and anguish. Witnesses described the dancers' expressions as a mix of pleasure and pain, their features contorted with a strange blend of ecstasy and suffering. It was as if the dance had become a conduit for the release of both elation and inner turmoil, an amalgamation of conflicting emotions that mirrored the complexities of the human psyche.

The dance of the afflicted was marked by uncontrolled movements and a distortion of the human form. Witnesses observed limbs jerking and twitching uncontrollably, bodies writhing and convulsing in a seemingly chaotic frenzy. The dance appeared to transcend the dancers' conscious control, as if their bodies had become vessels for a force beyond their comprehension. This lack of agency and the distorted physicality of the dancers added to the eerie and unsettling nature of the phenomenon.

Although the dance exhibited common characteristics among the afflicted, there were also variations in the styles and movements displayed. Some dancers spun in dizzying circles, their bodies whirling as if caught in a vortex. Others hopped and leaped with an unnatural agility, defying the boundaries of gravity. Some dancers engaged in wild gesticulations, their arms flailing and their hands contorting into intricate patterns. These variations in dance styles within the plague hinted at individuality amidst the collective frenzy, suggesting that the dance retained a fragment of personal expression within its seemingly chaotic nature.

The unrelenting nature of the dance took a toll on the dancers' bodies. As the hours turned into days, injuries began to manifest. Witnesses reported bloody and bruised feet from incessant movement, sprained joints from repetitive and forceful motions, and exhausted bodies pushed beyond their limits. The physical manifestations of the dance served as a testament to the immense strain and endurance required to sustain the frenzied movements. Yet, despite the injuries, the dancers pressed on, seemingly impervious to pain and the limitations of their own bodies.

The dance of the afflicted was not limited to the physical realm alone; it also manifested in the dancers' expressions and gaze. Witnesses observed contorted facial features, with grimaces, wide-eyed stares, and twisted mouths. It was as if the dance had penetrated deep into their souls, distorting their very beings. The dancers' eyes, in particular, held a haunting quality, oscillating between vacant and wild, as if their gaze had been consumed by the all-consuming dance.

Accompanying the physical movements were vocalizations and sounds emitted by the dancers. Witnesses reported a cacophony of cries, screams, laughter, and incomprehensible utterances. These vocal expressions ranged from joyous outbursts to anguished wails, adding another layer of complexity to the overall experience of the dance. The sounds seemed to echo the internal tumult within the dancers, amplifying the sensory intensity of the plague and leaving a haunting impression on those who bore witness.

Despite the physical and emotional challenges posed by the dance, some witnesses noted a sense of catharsis and liberation in the afflicted individuals. The dance seemed to serve as a vessel for the release of pent-up emotions and societal constraints, providing an outlet for personal expression in a society that often stifled individuality. For those caught in the grip of the dance, it offered a temporary respite from the burdens of daily life, a momentary escape into a realm of uninhibited movement and self-expression.

The dance of the afflicted left an indelible mark on the artistic consciousness of the time. Paintings, drawings, and literary works emerged, attempting to capture the essence of the dance and its profound impact. Artists sought to convey the frenetic energy, the contorted bodies, and the emotional depth embedded within the dance. These artistic interpretations provide glimpses into the visceral and visual aspects of the phenomenon, offering additional insights into its significance and portrayal.

In modern times, scientific analysis and contemporary perspectives have shed further light on the dance of the afflicted. Medical professionals, psychologists, and cultural historians have delved into the physical and psychological aspects of the phenomenon, offering theories and interpretations that bridge the gap between the past and the present. Their research and insights contribute to a deeper understanding of the dance and its implications within the broader context of human behavior and collective experiences.

Chapter Four

The Dancing Plague of 1518, initially confined to the streets of Strasbourg, began to spill over its boundaries, spreading like wildfire to neighboring towns and villages. In this chapter, we delve into the mechanisms that facilitated the rapid spread of the plague, exploring the factors that contributed to its contagious nature and examining the far-reaching consequences it had on the region.

One of the primary modes of transmission for the dancing plague was through sight and sound. Witnesses who observed the afflicted individuals in the throes of the dance found themselves inexplicably drawn to join, as if an invisible force compelled them to participate. The frenzied movements and sounds emitted by the dancers seemed to trigger a chain reaction, luring in new participants and perpetuating the spread of the plague. The contagious nature of the dance highlighted the profound influence that visual and auditory stimuli can have on human behavior.

Beyond the physical transmission, the dancing plague also spread through social contagion and mass hysteria. As word of the outbreak spread, communities were gripped by fear and curiosity, leading individuals to seek out the spectacle and inadvertently become part of it. The collective frenzy and communal atmosphere surrounding the dance created an environment conducive to the rapid transmission of the plague. It served as a stark reminder of the power of group dynamics and the influence of social context on individual behavior.

The cultural practices and rituals prevalent in the region played a significant role in the spread of the plague. Strasbourg and its surrounding towns had a rich tradition of communal celebrations, religious processions, and festivities. These gatherings, characterized by music, dance, and ecstatic rituals, provided fertile ground for the transmission of the dancing plague. The lines between the customary and the pathological became blurred, as the boundaries of acceptable behavior and expression became distorted in the face of the plague's relentless spread.

The geographical location of Strasbourg, positioned at the crossroads of major trade routes, contributed to the swift dissemination of the dancing plague. The city acted as a hub for commerce, attracting merchants, travelers, and pilgrims from near and far. As they ventured out of Strasbourg, carrying tales of the strange and captivating dance, they unknowingly became carriers of the contagion, unwittingly spreading it to new communities and regions along their journeys.

As the plague continued its relentless march, panic gripped the affected towns and villages. Communities resorted to desperate measures, attempting to isolate themselves from the source of the contagion. Quarantine measures were put in place, with afflicted individuals and suspected carriers sequestered in designated areas. However, these efforts often proved futile, as the dancing plague defied conventional containment methods and continued to surge through the region.

The spread of the dancing plague had far-reaching consequences for the trade and economy of the affected areas. As towns and villages grappled with the outbreak, commerce and daily transactions came to a grinding halt. Merchants and traders, fearful of contracting the plague, avoided the afflicted regions, disrupting the flow of goods and services. The economic repercussions compounded the social and psychological turmoil, exacerbating the sense of unease and uncertainty that permeated the communities.

As the dancing plague engulfed multiple towns and villages, regional authorities were compelled to take collective action. Meetings and consultations were held to devise strategies to combat the spread and mitigate the impact of the plague. Regional officials coordinated efforts to share information, implement quarantine measures, and pool resources to address the crisis. This unprecedented collaboration demonstrated the recognition of the shared threat and the necessity for a unified response.

In the face of the spreading plague, religious authorities played a crucial role in attempting to stem its tide. Clergy members organized processions, prayers, and supplications, seeking divine intervention to halt the dance and alleviate the suffering of the afflicted. Religious rituals and spiritual practices became a focal point for communities grappling with the inexplicable phenomenon. The collective faith and fervent appeals to higher powers were a testament to the lengths people would go to find solace and a sense of hope amidst the chaos.

As the plague continued its relentless march, fear and social stigmatization began to intensify. Communities viewed the afflicted with a mix of fascination, pity, and trepidation. The dancing individuals were often ostracized and treated as outcasts, regarded with suspicion and fear. The fear of contagion permeated social interactions, further isolating the afflicted and exacerbating the psychological toll on both individuals and communities.

While the dancing plague spread through multiple towns and villages, it also exhibited variations in its manifestation and impact across different regions. Local beliefs, superstitions, and cultural practices shaped the understanding and response to the plague. Some communities interpreted the dance as a form of divine punishment, while others attributed it to malevolent forces or witchcraft. These varied interpretations contributed to the complexity of the phenomenon and highlighted the interplay between local beliefs and the collective response to the outbreak.

Despite the initial challenges, the dancing plague eventually began to subside, its fervor waning as abruptly as it had emerged. The reasons for its eventual containment remain shrouded in mystery. Some speculate that physical exhaustion and the gradual passing of time played a role, while others attribute its decline to psychological and social factors. Regardless, the plague's eventual containment brought a collective sigh of relief, even as the scars of its impact remained etched in the collective memory.

The spread of the dancing plague left a lasting cultural legacy in the affected regions. The traumatic experience and the social upheaval brought about by the plague led to shifts in cultural practices, religious beliefs, and societal norms. It prompted reflections on the fragility of human existence and the limits of human understanding. The memory of the dancing plague endured, serving as a cautionary tale and a reminder of the unpredictability of life and the extraordinary resilience of human communities.

The dancing plague of 1518 continues to captivate the imagination and intrigue scholars to this day. It serves as a reminder of the intricacies of human behavior, the power of collective phenomena, and the enduring questions that surround the human mind and its susceptibility to contagion. The lessons learned from the spread of the plague have informed our understanding of historical epidemics and continue to resonate in contemporary discussions on public health, psychology, and societal dynamics.

Chapter Five

The Dancing Plague of 1518 presented a baffling phenomenon that defied conventional medical and religious understanding. In this chapter, we delve into the medical and religious explanations that were put forth at the time to make sense of the plague. We explore the theories proposed by physicians, scholars, and religious authorities, attempting to unravel the mysteries that surrounded this extraordinary event.

In the medical realm, prevailing theories of the time sought to explain the dancing plague through the lens of ancient medical concepts. Physicians attributed the outbreak to miasma, a noxious form of air believed to carry disease. They posited that the afflicted individuals had been exposed to a toxic atmosphere that disrupted the delicate balance of bodily humors, leading to the uncontrollable dance. This explanation reflected the prevailing medical knowledge of the era, rooted in the teachings of Hippocrates and Galen.

Religious authorities offered a different perspective, interpreting the dancing plague as a manifestation of supernatural possession or demonic influence. They saw the afflicted individuals as vessels for malevolent spirits, driven to dance against their will. Exorcisms and religious rituals were performed in attempts to cast out the perceived evil forces and alleviate the suffering of the afflicted. The religious explanation highlighted the belief in the spiritual realm and the power of divine intervention in the face of inexplicable phenomena.

A significant religious figure associated with the dancing plague was Saint Vitus, a Christian martyr known for his healing abilities. The belief in the intercession of Saint Vitus gained prominence during the outbreak, with many attributing the dancing plague to his influence. The phenomenon became commonly known as the Dance of Saint Vitus, solidifying the connection between the plague and the saint. This religious association provided a framework for understanding and seeking solace in the midst of the widespread affliction.

In more recent times, medical experts have revisited the dancing plague from a psychological perspective. They propose that the outbreak was a manifestation of mass psychogenic illness, commonly known as mass hysteria. This theory suggests that the contagious nature of the dance, coupled with social and psychological factors, triggered a collective psychological response in susceptible individuals, resulting in the mass adoption of the dance. The power of suggestion and the amplification of symptoms through social dynamics played a central role in this explanation.

Another medical explanation that has gained traction in modern research is ergotism, a condition caused by the ingestion of rye contaminated with the ergot fungus. Ergotism can lead to hallucinations, spasms, and other neurological symptoms that closely resemble the manifestations of the dancing plague. Some researchers suggest that the consumption of contaminated food, such as bread made from infected grain, could have contributed to the outbreak. This theory aligns with the historical context of the region, known for its reliance on rye as a staple crop.

Medical and religious explanations aside, sociocultural factors and collective behavior also played a significant role in the dancing plague. The social context of the time, characterized by religious fervor, communal celebrations, and cultural practices, provided a fertile ground for the contagion to take hold. The power of suggestion, social conformity, and the desire for communal belonging influenced the behavior of individuals, contributing to the rapid spread and continuation of the plague.

While medical and religious explanations of the dancing plague often appeared at odds with each other, there were instances where these explanations overlapped or intersected. Some physicians acknowledged the potential influence of supernatural forces in the manifestation of the plague, while religious authorities recognized the physical toll and bodily afflictions experienced by the dancers. This interplay between medical and religious explanations reflects the complexity of human understanding in attempting to make sense of a phenomenon that defied easy categorization.

The medical and religious explanations of the dancing plague sparked intense public discourse and debates among scholars, intellectuals, and the general population. Physicians, theologians, and philosophers engaged in lively exchanges, presenting their arguments and counterarguments, attempting to reconcile the scientific and spiritual aspects of the phenomenon. These debates contributed to the intellectual and cultural landscape of the time, highlighting the quest for knowledge and understanding in the face of the inexplicable.

To fully comprehend the medical and religious explanations of the dancing plague, it is essential to consider the historical context and paradigm shifts of the era. The outbreak occurred during a time of significant intellectual and scientific transformation, with the Renaissance challenging long-held beliefs and ushering in a new era of exploration and inquiry. The clash between traditional medical theories rooted in ancient wisdom and emerging scientific perspectives created a fertile ground for debates and the evolution of understanding.

In the modern era, with advances in medical and psychological knowledge, scholars continue to revisit the dancing plague, offering new interpretations and perspectives. The explanations put forth in contemporary research draw from a multidisciplinary approach, incorporating medical, psychological, sociological, and cultural factors. However, the inherent limitations of studying a historical event present challenges in definitively determining the exact cause or explanation of the dancing plague, leaving room for ongoing speculation and debate.

Regardless of the specific medical or religious explanations, the dancing plague holds a significant cultural significance and symbolism. It serves as a powerful metaphor for the complexities of human behavior, the mysteries of the mind, and the fragile boundary between the individual and the collective. The enduring legacy of the dancing plague resides not only in the historical records but also in its symbolic resonance, reminding us of the human capacity for both extraordinary expression and vulnerability to contagion.

The medical and religious explanations of the dancing plague offer valuable lessons and insights that remain relevant in contemporary contexts. They underscore the importance of interdisciplinary approaches to understanding complex phenomena, the need for open dialogue and collaboration among different fields of knowledge, and the recognition of the profound interplay between the physical, psychological, and social dimensions of human experience. The dancing plague serves as a reminder of the enduring quest for understanding and the inherent limitations of our comprehension.

Chapter Six

In this chapter, we delve into the theories and speculations surrounding the dancing plague of 1518. As a phenomenon that defies easy explanation, numerous hypotheses have been put forth over the years to shed light on the underlying causes. We explore various perspectives, ranging from psychological factors to environmental influences, as we attempt to unravel the mysteries of this extraordinary event.

One prominent theory suggests that the dancing plague was a manifestation of mass hysteria, also known as mass psychogenic illness. According to this view, the contagious nature of the dance, coupled with social dynamics and the power of suggestion, triggered a collective psychological response in susceptible individuals. The dance spread through social networks, fueling a cycle of imitation and amplification. This theory highlights the influence of social contagion and the role of psychological factors in shaping collective behavior.

Another line of speculation explores the cultural and societal influences that may have contributed to the outbreak of the dancing plague. The social and cultural context of the time, characterized by religious fervor, communal celebrations, and cultural practices, provided a fertile ground for the contagion to take hold. The convergence of religious rituals, traditional dances, and heightened emotional states may have acted as catalysts, amplifying the spread and continuation of the dance. This perspective emphasizes the interplay between cultural practices and collective behavior.

Some researchers propose that economic and social stressors played a role in the dancing plague. The region at the time experienced economic hardships, with poverty, famine, and social unrest prevailing. It is suggested that the dance served as a physical and psychological release valve for individuals experiencing stress and hardship, offering temporary relief from the challenges of daily life. This theory highlights the potential link between socioeconomic factors and the manifestation of collective behavior.

Ergotism, a condition caused by the ingestion of rye contaminated with the ergot fungus, has been put forward as a possible explanation for the dancing plague. Ergot alkaloids found in the fungus can induce hallucinations, convulsions, and spasms, resembling the symptoms exhibited by the dancers. It is hypothesized that the consumption of contaminated food, such as bread made from infected grain, may have contributed to the outbreak. This theory aligns with the historical context of the region, known for its reliance on rye as a staple crop.

Another speculative perspective examines the psychological triggers and trauma experienced by the dancers. It is suggested that the combination of physical, emotional, and societal stressors may have pushed individuals to a breaking point, resulting in a dissociative state that manifested as the uncontrollable dance. This theory emphasizes the role of psychological trauma and the potential for extreme stress to induce unusual and involuntary physical expressions.

Environmental factors and contaminants have also been proposed as contributing factors to the dancing plague. The region where the outbreak occurred was known to be susceptible to various environmental toxins and contaminants, including heavy metals and water pollution. It is hypothesized that exposure to such substances may have had neurological effects, leading to the dance-like movements. This theory highlights the potential impact of environmental factors on human health and behavior.

Throughout history, supernatural and religious interpretations have been intertwined with attempts to explain the dancing plague. Some theories suggest that the dance was a form of divine punishment or a result of demonic influence. These interpretations view the phenomenon through a spiritual lens, attributing it to supernatural forces. They emphasize the belief in the interplay between the spiritual and physical realms, with the dance serving as a visible manifestation of divine or demonic presence. These interpretations highlight the enduring influence of religious beliefs and the human tendency to seek supernatural explanations for extraordinary events.

Given the complexity of the dancing plague, many researchers propose a combination of multiple factors as the most plausible explanation. They argue that no single theory can fully account for all aspects of the phenomenon. Instead, a convergence of psychological, social, cultural, environmental, and physiological factors likely played a role in the outbreak. This integrative perspective recognizes the multifaceted nature of human behavior and the interconnectedness of various influences.

To gain a deeper understanding of the dancing plague, it is crucial to examine its historical context and compare it with similar instances of mass hysteria or collective behavior. By studying other cases throughout history, such as the Tarantism phenomenon in Southern Italy or the Tanganyika laughter epidemic, researchers can draw parallels and identify commonalities in the underlying factors that contribute to such outbreaks. This comparative approach provides valuable insights into the broader dynamics of collective behavior.

Retrospective analysis of the dancing plague faces inherent limitations due to the scarcity of historical records and the challenge of interpreting events from a distance. Researchers must rely on fragmented accounts and subjective descriptions, making it difficult to definitively determine the true cause of the phenomenon. Despite these limitations, modern scholars continue to explore and speculate on the theories surrounding the dancing plague, pushing the boundaries of knowledge and understanding.

The theories and speculations surrounding the dancing plague have broader implications for contemporary society. They highlight the potential for collective behavior, mass psychogenic illness, and social contagion in modern contexts. Understanding the underlying factors that contribute to such phenomena can inform public health strategies, crisis management, and the prevention of the spread of unfounded beliefs or behaviors. Lessons from the dancing plague emphasize the importance of interdisciplinary approaches and the integration of medical, psychological, sociological, and cultural perspectives.

As researchers explore theories and speculations surrounding the dancing plague, it is essential to address ethical considerations. The potential for stigmatization, sensationalism, or the exploitation of vulnerable populations must be acknowledged and mitigated. Ethical guidelines and rigorous research practices are necessary to ensure that investigations into the dancing plague or similar events are conducted with respect, integrity, and a commitment to the well-being of individuals and communities.

Chapter Seven

In this chapter, we delve into the social and cultural factors that played a significant role in the dancing plague of 1518. Examining the societal context, prevailing beliefs, and cultural practices of the time provides valuable insights into the collective behavior and the spread of the phenomenon. By understanding the social and cultural dynamics at play, we can unravel the complexities of the dancing plague and its impact on the affected communities.

Religion held immense influence during the 16th century, and it shaped the social fabric of communities. The dancing plague occurred in a deeply religious era, where religious beliefs and practices permeated every aspect of life. The intense religious fervor, rituals, and processions provided a fertile ground for the outbreak to take hold. The supernatural interpretations of the dancing plague and the search for divine intervention reflect the deeply ingrained religious mindset of the time.

Religious institutions played a central role in the response to the dancing plague. Church authorities, clergy, and religious leaders were instrumental in shaping public opinion and directing the actions taken to address the phenomenon. They interpreted the dance through the lens of religious doctrines, seeking to understand the spiritual meaning and significance behind the bizarre behavior. The involvement of religious institutions further fueled the cultural and societal impact of the dancing plague.

Superstitions and folk beliefs were prevalent during the 16th century, permeating the daily lives of individuals. People held a deep belief in supernatural forces, witchcraft, and the influence of curses. Such beliefs created an environment conducive to the spread of rumors, attributing the dancing plague to witchcraft, demonic possession, or divine punishment. The intertwining of superstitions with the dancing plague shaped public perception and influenced collective responses to the phenomenon.

The occurrence of the dancing plague coincided with festivals, celebrations, and communal gatherings in the region. These events brought together large groups of people, fostering a sense of collective identity and shared experiences. The convergence of festivities and the heightened emotional states during such occasions may have contributed to the rapid transmission of the dance. The social cohesion and shared cultural practices amplified the impact of the dancing plague within affected communities.

Dance held a significant place in the cultural fabric of the 16th-century society. It served as a form of expression, communication, and communal bonding. Dance was deeply ingrained in religious rituals, festive celebrations, and social interactions. The dance in the dancing plague was a departure from the joyful and purposeful dances of the time, transforming into a compulsive and uncontrollable act. The perversion of dance disrupted the familiar social order, challenging the cultural norms and expectations surrounding this art form.

The dancing plague exemplifies the power of collective behavior and social contagion. The contagious nature of the dance, both in terms of physical movement and social influence, led to the rapid spread of the phenomenon within and across communities. The shared experiences, heightened emotions, and the desire for social cohesion fueled the perpetuation of the dance. The collective nature of the behavior intensified the impact of the dancing plague and contributed to its social and cultural significance.

Social hierarchies and power dynamics influenced the response to the dancing plague. The affected individuals came from different social backgrounds, but during the dance, social distinctions blurred, and a sense of equality prevailed. The disruption of social norms challenged the established power structures, creating both opportunities and challenges for those in positions of authority. The dance broke down barriers and created a sense of unity among the afflicted, leading to a temporary shift in social dynamics. This shift in power challenged the existing social order and had profound implications for the affected communities.

Gender dynamics and societal expectations played a significant role in the dancing plague. The majority of those affected by the dance were women, and their participation in the phenomenon challenged prevailing gender roles and norms. Women, who were expected to be submissive and controlled in their behavior, engaged in uninhibited and uncontrollable movements during the dance. The disruption of gender expectations further heightened the societal impact of the dancing plague.

The dancing plague tested the social fabric of the affected communities. As the dance spread, fear, confusion, and distrust permeated the social interactions. The dance created a climate of uncertainty and anxiety, leading to the breakdown of social cohesion and trust. The communal bonds that once held the communities together were strained, as individuals sought to protect themselves from the contagious dance. The erosion of trust had lasting effects on the affected communities.

Rumors and public opinion played a significant role in shaping the response to the dancing plague. In the absence of concrete scientific explanations, rumors flourished, attributing the dance to various supernatural, demonic, or religious causes. Public opinion swayed between fear, fascination, and attempts to rationalize the phenomenon. The influence of rumors and public discourse further amplified the social and cultural impact of the dancing plague.

Local authorities were tasked with managing the outbreak and mitigating its impact on the affected communities. Their responses ranged from attempts to contain the dance through quarantine and isolation to organizing religious processions and ceremonies. Local authorities sought to restore order, alleviate public fears, and provide a sense of control in the face of a baffling phenomenon. The effectiveness of these responses varied, highlighting the challenges faced by the authorities in dealing with a novel and unprecedented event.

The individuals who survived the dancing plague faced significant challenges upon their reintegration into society. They often encountered stigma, social exclusion, and even accusations of being witches or possessed by evil spirits. The process of reintegration was complex, requiring efforts to rebuild trust, dispel misconceptions, and address the psychological and social consequences of the dance. The stigmatization and social exclusion experienced by the survivors left a lasting impact on their lives.

The dancing plague left a profound cultural and social imprint on the affected communities. It challenged traditional beliefs, disrupted social order, and created a rupture in the collective memory. The event became ingrained in local folklore and shaped cultural narratives for generations to come. The legacy of the dancing plague serves as a reminder of the complex interplay between social, cultural, and psychological factors in shaping collective behavior.

Chapter Eight

In this chapter, we delve into the various responses and interventions undertaken by local authorities, religious institutions, and medical practitioners in the face of the dancing plague of 1518. The unprecedented nature of the phenomenon presented significant challenges, and the actions taken to address the outbreak varied in their effectiveness and approach. Examining these responses provides valuable insights into the prevailing beliefs, societal attitudes, and medical practices of the time.

Local authorities were at the forefront of managing the dancing plague outbreak. They were responsible for maintaining public order, safeguarding the well-being of the community, and containing the spread of the dance. Measures such as quarantine, isolation, and attempts to enforce control over the affected individuals were implemented. This section explores the role and challenges faced by local authorities in dealing with a baffling and uncontrollable phenomenon.

Religious institutions played a prominent role in responding to the dancing plague. The clergy, as intermediaries between the divine and the people, were expected to provide guidance, comfort, and spiritual solace. Religious ceremonies, processions, and prayers were organized to seek divine intervention and alleviate the dance. The influence of religious institutions in shaping public opinion and the response to the phenomenon is examined in this section.

Medical practitioners of the time grappled with the mystery of the dancing plague and sought to provide medical explanations and interventions. Physicians, healers, and local medical authorities approached the phenomenon through the lens of contemporary medical knowledge and practices. This section explores the medical theories and treatments employed, ranging from bloodletting and herbal remedies to the use of incantations and charms.

In the absence of a clear understanding of the cause of the dancing plague, various rational explanations were put forth by scholars, intellectuals, and observers of the time. These explanations sought to find logical and scientific reasons for the dance, such as imbalances of bodily humors, astrological influences, or environmental factors. This section explores the attempts made to provide rational explanations and the impact of these theories on the response to the phenomenon.

As the dancing plague spread, measures of containment and isolation were implemented to prevent further transmission. Quarantine areas were established, and the affected individuals were separated from the general population. This section examines the effectiveness of these measures, the challenges faced in their implementation, and the impact on the lives of those subjected to isolation.

The psychological and emotional well-being of the afflicted individuals and the community at large were crucial considerations in the response to the dancing plague. Efforts were made to provide support, comfort, and reassurance to those affected. This section explores the role of emotional support, the use of music and calming rituals, and the impact of communal solidarity on the mental health of the individuals involved.

The dancing plague had profound social and economic repercussions for the affected communities. This section examines the disruptions caused by the dance in everyday life, including the suspension of work, trade, and commerce. The economic impact on individuals, families, and the broader society is explored, shedding light on the far-reaching consequences of the phenomenon.

The effectiveness of the responses and interventions to the dancing plague varied, and their evaluation provides valuable insights. This section critically examines the strengths and weaknesses of the measures undertaken, the cultural and societal biases that influenced decision-making, and the lessons learned from the response to the outbreak. Reflecting on the responses and interventions implemented during the dancing plague allows us to assess their effectiveness in containing the outbreak and mitigating its impact. This evaluation takes into account the contextual factors, limitations of medical knowledge at the time, and the complexities of addressing a phenomenon as enigmatic as the dancing plague. By critically examining the response strategies, we can gain insights into the strengths and weaknesses of the approaches taken.

The response to the dancing plague raises important ethical considerations and highlights the humanitarian efforts undertaken. The treatment of the afflicted individuals, their social ostracization, and the attempts to provide care and support are examined in this section. It explores the moral and ethical dimensions of the response, shedding light on the compassion, empathy, or lack thereof, exhibited towards the affected individuals.

In the face of an unprecedented phenomenon like the dancing plague, cultural adaptations and ritualistic responses played a significant role. This section explores the development of specific rituals, dances, or ceremonies aimed at appeasing the divine or warding off the dance. It delves into the cultural significance of these adaptations and their impact on the affected communities.

The response to the dancing plague necessitated collaboration and the exchange of knowledge between different actors. This section explores the interactions between local authorities, religious institutions, and medical practitioners in their attempts to understand, manage, and ultimately control the outbreak. It examines the sharing of information, expertise, and experiences in a collective effort to combat the dance.

The dancing plague holds valuable lessons for understanding and responding to collective behavior and mass psychogenic illnesses. This section reflects on the historical legacy of the phenomenon, the insights gained from studying its response, and the relevance of these lessons to contemporary challenges. It highlights the importance of interdisciplinary approaches and the need for empathy, understanding, and evidence-based interventions in addressing such extraordinary events.

Comparing the response to the dancing plague with other epidemics and collective phenomena provides a broader perspective. This section draws parallels and contrasts with other instances of mass hysteria, contagion, or collective behavior, examining the similarities and unique aspects of the dancing plague. By situating the response within a comparative framework, we can gain a deeper understanding of the dynamics at play during extraordinary events.

Chapter Nine

In this chapter, we delve into the profound impact that the dancing plague of 1518 had on the daily lives of the affected communities. The relentless and uncontrollable dance disrupted every aspect of daily life, including work, family, social interactions, and cultural practices. Understanding the far-reaching consequences of the phenomenon sheds light on the challenges faced by individuals and communities in the face of such an extraordinary event.

The dancing plague caused significant economic disruption in the affected towns and regions. With individuals compelled to dance for days or even weeks, work came to a halt. Fields remained unattended, workshops were abandoned, and businesses suffered. This section explores the economic consequences of the dance, including loss of productivity, trade disruptions, and long-term economic repercussions.

The dance had a profound impact on social and family life. Families were torn apart as loved ones succumbed to the dance, leaving behind grieving relatives. Social gatherings, festivities, and communal activities were disrupted, as the dance consumed the thoughts and energy of the afflicted individuals. This section examines the strain on social relationships, the emotional toll on families, and the challenges of maintaining social bonds in the midst of the dance.

The dancing plague challenged traditional gender roles and dynamics of the time. The majority of those affected by the dance were women, and their participation in the phenomenon upended societal expectations. Women, who were expected to be subservient and controlled in their behavior, engaged in uninhibited and uncontrollable movements during the dance. This section explores the impact on women's roles, gender dynamics, and the societal response to their participation in the dance.

Cultural practices and festivals held great significance in the affected communities, but the dancing plague disrupted these cherished traditions. The dance overshadowed religious ceremonies, disrupted annual festivals, and forced the cancellation of cultural events. This section examines the loss of cultural heritage, the impact on communal identity, and the challenges of preserving traditions in the midst of the dance.

Religion and spirituality played a significant role in the lives of the affected communities, but the dancing plague had a profound impact on religious observance. The dance eclipsed religious rituals, processions, and prayers, creating a spiritual void. This section explores the challenges faced by religious institutions, the crisis of faith experienced by individuals, and the attempts to reconcile the dance with religious beliefs.

The relentless and uncontrollable nature of the dance had severe psychological and emotional consequences for the individuals involved. Fear, anxiety, and despair pervaded the minds of the afflicted, while confusion and helplessness engulfed the community. This section examines the psychological trauma experienced by the dancers, the emotional toll on the broader population, and the long-term psychological consequences of the phenomenon.

The dancing plague posed significant challenges to healthcare and medical services of the time. The lack of understanding surrounding the cause and treatment of the dance hindered effective medical intervention. This section explores the limitations of medical knowledge, the attempts made by physicians and healers to provide relief, and the impact of the dance on the healthcare system of the affected communities.

In the face of the dancing plague, communities rallied together to provide support and solidarity. Despite the challenges, acts of compassion, care, and empathy were witnessed. This section explores the role of community support networks, the formation of caretaking groups, and the resilience exhibited by the affected communities in the face of the dancing plague, communities rallied together to provide support and solidarity. Despite the challenges, acts of compassion, care, and empathy were witnessed. This section explores the role of community support networks, the formation of caretaking groups, and the resilience exhibited by the affected communities. It examines how neighbors, friends, and even strangers came together to assist the afflicted and their families, offering emotional support, practical assistance, and a sense of belonging in the midst of the dance.

While community support and solidarity were evident, the dancing plague also led to stigmatization and social ostracism of the afflicted individuals. The mysterious and uncontrollable nature of the dance fueled fear and suspicion, leading to isolation and exclusion. This section explores the social consequences faced by those affected, including the loss of social status, discrimination, and the challenges of reintegrating into society once the dance subsided.

Education and intellectual pursuits were severely disrupted during the dancing plague. Schools and universities were forced to close, interrupting the learning process for students. Intellectual activities, such as philosophical debates and scholarly discussions, took a backseat as the dance consumed the thoughts and attention of the affected communities. This section examines the impact on education, the disruption of intellectual life, and the long-term consequences on knowledge acquisition and dissemination.

The dancing plague influenced various forms of artistic expression, including art, music, and literature. Artists captured the haunting images of the dance in their works, musicians composed melodies inspired by the rhythms of the dance, and writers sought to make sense of the phenomenon through their narratives. This section explores the impact on artistic creativity, the emergence of new cultural expressions, and the ways in which the dance left an indelible mark on artistic representations of the time.

The dancing plague left a lasting imprint on the collective memory and identity of the affected communities. The stories, legends, and folklore passed down through generations kept the memory of the dance alive. This section examines how the dancing plague became part of the historical narrative, shaping the collective identity of the communities and contributing to their sense of uniqueness and resilience.

The dancing plague forced individuals and communities to reflect on their priorities and reevaluate their way of life. The fragility of human existence, the uncertainty of the future, and the transient nature of social norms were brought to the forefront. This section explores the introspection triggered by the dance, the reassessment of values and aspirations, and the lasting impact on personal and communal perspectives.

Chapter Ten

In this chapter, we explore the decline and eventual end of the dancing plague of 1518. After weeks of relentless dancing, the phenomenon began to subside, allowing the affected communities to gradually return to a semblance of normalcy. This chapter delves into the factors that contributed to the cessation of the dancing craze and the aftermath of the extraordinary event.

As the dancing plague persisted, there came a point when the number of new dance cases began to decline. The once-packed streets and squares emptied, and the dance became less prevalent. This section examines the gradual decrease in dance cases, exploring potential explanations for this decline and the impact it had on the affected communities.

One significant factor that contributed to the subsiding of the dancing craze was the physical and mental exhaustion experienced by the dancers. The relentless dancing took a toll on their bodies and minds, leading to fatigue, injuries, and psychological distress. This section explores the physical and mental challenges faced by the afflicted individuals and how exhaustion played a role in the decline of the dance.

The dancing plague triggered various psychological factors and behavioral changes among the affected individuals. Over time, the initial compulsion to dance began to wane, and individuals started to exhibit resistance to the dance. This section examines the psychological aspects of the dancing craze subsiding, including the psychological resilience of the dancers, the emergence of behavioral changes, and the psychological factors that contributed to the decline.

Throughout the dancing plague, various intervention and support measures were implemented to address the phenomenon. Local authorities, religious institutions, and medical practitioners offered assistance, care, and guidance to the affected communities. This section explores the impact of these intervention and support measures in facilitating the subsiding of the dancing craze and the role they played in helping individuals overcome the compulsion to dance.

As the dancing craze subsided, the challenge of community reintegration emerged. The affected individuals and their families had to navigate the social dynamics and stigma associated with the dance. This section explores the process of community reintegration, including the acceptance and support offered by the broader community, the struggles faced by the dancers, and the efforts made to rebuild social bonds.

The dancing plague had a significant socioeconomic impact on the affected communities. With the subsiding of the dance, the process of socioeconomic recovery began. This section examines the challenges faced in rebuilding the economy, restoring work activities, and addressing the long-term consequences of the dance on the economic stability of the towns and regions.

The subsiding of the dancing craze provided an opportunity for medical practitioners and scientists to reflect on the phenomenon. This section explores the medical and scientific reflections that emerged in the aftermath of the dance, including attempts to understand the cause of the phenomenon, the development of new medical knowledge, and the contributions of the dancing plague to the advancement of medical understanding.

The subsiding of the dancing craze allowed for the documentation and recording of the extraordinary event. Chroniclers, scholars, and eyewitnesses began to compile accounts, narratives, and historical records of the dancing plague. This section explores the historical documentation and accounts that provide valuable insights into the nature of the phenomenon, its impact, and the collective memory of the communities affected.

The dancing craze left a lasting legacy and cultural significance in the affected communities. This section explores the legacy and cultural significance of the dancing craze. It examines how the memory of the dance was preserved and passed down through generations, the ways in which it shaped local folklore and traditions, and its enduring impact on the cultural identity of the affected communities. Additionally, it explores the broader cultural significance of the dancing plague, including its representation in art, literature, and popular culture.

The subsiding of the dancing craze prompted interpretations and reflections on the phenomenon. Scholars, historians, and researchers sought to understand the deeper meanings and lessons to be gleaned from this extraordinary event. This section explores the various interpretations of the dancing plague, including sociocultural, psychological, and medical perspectives. It also reflects on the lessons learned from the dancing craze and their relevance to our understanding of collective behavior and historical phenomena.

The subsiding of the dancing craze marked the beginning of a period of recovery and rebuilding for the affected communities. This section examines the aftermath of the dance, including the physical, psychological, and societal recovery processes. It explores how the communities coped with the aftermath, rebuilt their lives, and sought to move forward in the wake of such a profound and transformative event.

Even after the subsiding of the dancing craze, controversies and debates surrounded the phenomenon. This section explores the ongoing discussions and differing opinions regarding the cause of the dance, ranging from medical explanations to supernatural and religious interpretations. It examines the controversies that emerged in the aftermath of the dance and the debates that continue to shape our understanding of this enigmatic historical event.

The subsiding of the dancing craze allows for a comparative analysis with other instances of mass hysteria and epidemic outbreaks. This section examines the similarities and differences between the dancing plague and other phenomena, such as the Salem Witch Trials, tarantism, and other dancing manias. It explores the shared characteristics, underlying factors, and societal responses to these collective phenomena.

Chapter Eleven

In this chapter, we explore the historical significance of the dancing plague of 1518 and the various interpretations it has garnered over the centuries. The extraordinary nature of the phenomenon and its lasting impact on the affected communities have sparked ongoing discussions and debates among scholars and historians. This chapter delves into the historical significance of the dancing plague and the diverse interpretations that shed light on its meaning and implications.

The dancing plague of 1518 marked a significant cultural and social moment in history. This section examines the ways in which the phenomenon brought about cultural and social transformations in the affected communities. It explores how the dance challenged existing social norms, disrupted traditional practices, and reshaped the collective identity of the communities. Additionally, it examines the long-term cultural shifts that occurred as a result of the dancing plague.

The dancing plague had implications for power and authority structures within the affected communities. This section explores the dynamics between the ruling authorities, religious institutions, and the afflicted individuals during the dance. It examines the responses of those in positions of power, their attempts to control or manage the phenomenon, and the challenges they faced in maintaining social order. Additionally, it analyzes the impact of the dancing plague on the perception of authority and its long-term consequences.

The dancing plague had significant economic consequences for the affected communities. This section explores the disruptions to labor and economic activities caused by the dance. It examines the impact on trade, production, and daily livelihoods. Additionally, it analyzes the ways in which the economic repercussions of the dancing plague shaped subsequent economic practices and policies in the region.

The dancing plague also shed light on gender and social roles within the affected communities. This section examines the gender dynamics at play during the dance, including the predominance of women among the afflicted and the societal expectations placed upon them. It explores the ways in which gender norms and social roles were challenged and renegotiated in the wake of the dancing plague, and the potential long-term effects on gender relations.

The dancing plague has been subject to various psychological and sociocultural explanations throughout history. This section explores the different interpretations put forth by scholars and historians. It examines psychological factors such as mass hysteria, collective behavior, and psychosocial stressors, as well as sociocultural factors such as religious beliefs, social unrest, and cultural anxieties. Additionally, it discusses the merits and limitations of each interpretation and their contribution to our understanding of the phenomenon.

The dancing plague also prompted medical perspectives and scientific advances in the field of medicine. This section examines the medical explanations and theories proposed by physicians and scholars of the time. It explores the understanding of diseases and mental health in the 16th century, the medical interventions attempted during the dancing plague, and the long-term impact on medical practices and knowledge.

The dancing plague has often been interpreted symbolically or allegorically. This section explores the symbolic meanings attributed to the dance, ranging from religious symbolism to social commentary. It examines how the dancing plague has been used as a metaphor for societal ills, political unrest, or spiritual crisis. Additionally, it discusses the implications of these symbolic interpretations for our understanding of the phenomenon.

The dancing plague has left a lasting imprint on the historical memory of the affected communities. This section explores the ways in which the dance has been remembered and commemorated throughout history. It examines the preservation of the historical memory of the dancing plague through oral traditions, written accounts, and commemorative practices. It also explores the ways in which the dance has been incorporated into local folklore, festivals, and cultural events. Additionally, it discusses the role of collective memory in shaping the interpretation and significance of the dancing plague over time.

Understanding the historical significance of the dancing plague requires placing it within its broader historical context. This section explores the socio-political, religious, and cultural climate of 16th-century Europe to provide a framework for interpreting the phenomenon. It examines the societal challenges and anxieties of the time, such as religious conflicts, economic disparities, and cultural transformations. Furthermore, it engages in a comparative analysis, exploring similar instances of mass hysteria or collective behavior in different historical periods and regions.

The dancing plague of 1518 offers valuable lessons that are still relevant today. This section reflects on the insights gained from the historical significance and interpretations of the phenomenon. It examines the implications for our understanding of collective behavior, the influence of sociocultural factors on individual and group psychology, and the impact of historical events on cultural memory and identity. Additionally, it discusses the relevance of these lessons for contemporary society and the study of human behavior.

Interpreting historical events, especially those as enigmatic as the dancing plague, requires ethical considerations. This section explores the ethical dimensions of interpreting the phenomenon and its historical significance. It discusses the potential biases, cultural assumptions, and limitations that can influence interpretations. Additionally, it emphasizes the importance of interdisciplinary approaches, diverse perspectives, and responsible historical scholarship in understanding and representing the dancing plague.

Despite centuries of scholarly inquiry, the dancing plague still holds unanswered questions and avenues for further research. This section explores the gaps in our understanding of the phenomenon and identifies potential areas for future investigation. It highlights the need for interdisciplinary collaborations, advanced scientific methodologies, and access to historical records to shed further light on the historical significance and interpretations of the dancing plague.

Chapter Twelve

In this chapter, we explore the dancing plague of 1518 in the context of other epidemic outbreaks and instances of mass hysteria throughout history. By comparing the dancing plague with similar phenomena, we can gain a broader understanding of the underlying factors, societal responses, and long-term implications of these collective events. This chapter delves into the comparative analysis of the dancing plague and other epidemics, shedding light on the shared characteristics, unique features, and historical lessons they offer.

One of the most well-known instances of mass hysteria is the Salem Witch Trials of 1692-1693 in colonial Massachusetts. This section examines the similarities and differences between the dancing plague and the witch trials. It explores the social and cultural contexts, the role of religious beliefs and superstition, the collective anxieties, and the consequences for the affected communities. Additionally, it discusses the lessons learned from both events regarding the dangers of groupthink, scapegoating, and the impact of fear on individual and collective behavior.

Tarantism, a phenomenon characterized by uncontrollable dancing and other physical symptoms, emerged in Southern Italy during the 15th to 17th centuries. This section compares the dancing plague with tarantism, examining the similarities in the physical manifestations, the social and cultural contexts, and the religious interpretations of both phenomena. It explores the role of music and dance in the rituals associated with tarantism and their potential therapeutic effects. Additionally, it analyzes the differing sociocultural factors that contributed to the emergence and persistence of the dancing plague and tarantism.

Cholera outbreaks in the 19th century were often accompanied by social unrest and riots. This section explores the comparisons between the dancing plague and the cholera riots, focusing on the societal responses to both events. It examines the expressions of anger, fear, and frustration that led to collective violence during cholera outbreaks and the dancing plague. It also discusses the underlying factors, such as socioeconomic disparities and perceived injustices, that contributed to the outbreaks of violence. Furthermore, it reflects on the significance of these comparisons for our understanding of the relationship between epidemics, social unrest, and public health.

Ergotism, caused by the consumption of grain contaminated with the fungus Claviceps purpurea, led to outbreaks characterized by hallucinations, convulsions, and dancing manias. This section compares the dancing plague with ergotism, also known as St. Anthony's Fire. It explores the shared symptoms, including the compulsion to dance, the physical manifestations, and the psychological effects. It also examines the historical contexts, such as the prevalence of ergot-contaminated grain during the dancing plague and its association with religious practices. Additionally, it discusses the medical explanations and treatments for ergotism and their potential relevance to the dancing plague.

Mass hysteria continues to manifest in various forms in modern times. This section explores contemporary instances of collective behavior, such as the Tanganyika laughter epidemic in 1962, the Satanic Panic of the 1980s, and the internet-fueled outbreaks of psychogenic illness. It examines the similarities and differences between these events and the dancing plague, highlighting the role of media, social dynamics, and cultural factors in their occurrence. Furthermore, it discusses the insights gained from these comparisons for our understanding of mass hysteria in the modern world.

Comparing the dancing plague with other epidemics and instances of mass hysteria allows us to examine the societal responses to these events. This section explores the ways in which different societies have reacted to collective outbreaks. It examines the role of authorities, religious institutions, and medical practitioners in addressing and managing the phenomena. It also discusses the influence of cultural beliefs, political dynamics, and social structures on the responses, including the implementation of containment measures, the attribution of causation, and the provision of support and treatment to the affected individuals. Furthermore, it reflects on the lessons learned from historical and contemporary responses and their implications for future epidemic management.

Comparisons with other epidemics and instances of mass hysteria can provide insights into the long-term implications and legacies of these events. This section explores the lasting effects on the affected communities, including the social, cultural, and psychological consequences. It examines how collective traumas and stigmatization can persist, how cultural memory and identity are shaped, and how these events become embedded in the collective consciousness. Additionally, it discusses the potential positive outcomes, such as social change, increased awareness of mental health issues, and the advancement of scientific understanding.

The comparative analysis of the dancing plague and other epidemics offers valuable lessons for our understanding of collective behavior and epidemic management. This section reflects on the insights gained from these comparisons and their implications for future considerations. It discusses the importance of interdisciplinary approaches, the recognition of sociocultural factors, and the need for effective communication and collaboration among various stakeholders. Furthermore, it emphasizes the ongoing need for research, preparedness, and the promotion of mental health and well-being in times of epidemic outbreaks.

Chapter Thirteen

In this chapter, we delve into the psychological and sociological dimensions of the dancing plague of 1518. By exploring these perspectives, we can gain insights into the individual and collective factors that contributed to the phenomenon. This chapter examines the psychological processes underlying the manifestation of the dancing plague and analyzes the sociological dynamics that shaped its occurrence and spread. By integrating psychological and sociological perspectives, we aim to deepen our understanding of the complex interplay between individual experiences and social contexts.

This section focuses on the individual psychological experiences of those affected by the dancing plague. It explores the psychological factors that contributed to the compulsion to dance and the emotional and cognitive aspects of the phenomenon. It examines the potential role of stress, anxiety, and altered states of consciousness in the manifestation of the dancing plague. Additionally, it explores the psychological implications for the individuals involved, including the potential long-term effects on mental health and well-being.

The dancing plague of 1518 is a prime example of collective behavior, where individuals engage in similar actions without explicit coordination. This section delves into the sociological concept of social contagion, which explains the spread of behavior and emotions within a group. It explores how social contagion may have played a role in the transmission and perpetuation of the dancing plague. It also discusses the influence of social norms, group dynamics, and the power of suggestion in shaping collective behavior.

Cultural scripts and symbolic meanings play a crucial role in shaping collective behavior. This section examines the cultural and symbolic dimensions of the dancing plague. It explores how cultural beliefs, rituals, and social norms contributed to the understanding and interpretation of the phenomenon. It investigates the symbolic meanings attached to the act of dancing and the cultural context that gave rise to specific interpretations of the event. Additionally, it discusses how cultural scripts influenced the behaviors and responses of both the afflicted individuals and the wider community.

Social and collective identities influence individual and group behavior. This section explores the role of social and collective identities in the dancing plague. It examines how the identities of the affected individuals, such as their gender, occupation, and social status, may have shaped their experiences and responses. It also explores the formation of a collective identity among the affected community and the impact of this shared identity on their behaviors, beliefs, and interactions. Furthermore, it discusses the influence of social roles, power dynamics, and social hierarchies on the manifestation and interpretation of the dancing plague.

Explanatory models and attribution processes provide insights into how individuals make sense of and attribute meaning to their experiences. This section explores the diverse explanatory models and attribution processes that emerged during the dancing plague. It examines the medical, religious, and supernatural explanations offered by both the affected individuals and the wider society. It also discusses the social and psychological factors that influenced the acceptance or rejection of these explanations. Additionally, it reflects on the implications of attribution processes for understanding the dynamics of collective behavior and the social construction of reality.

Social support and coping mechanisms are crucial in times of collective crises. This section examines the role of social support networks and coping mechanisms in the context of the dancing plague. It explores how individuals and communities provided support and assistance to the affected individuals. It also discusses the various coping mechanisms employed by the afflicted, such as engaging in communal dances, seeking comfort in religious practices, or relying on social solidarity. Additionally, it reflects on the importance of social cohesion, interpersonal relationships, and communal rituals in providing a sense of stability, comfort, and resilience during the dancing plague.

The concept of the social amplification of risk helps us understand how societal factors contribute to the escalation and perpetuation of collective behavior. This section explores how social amplification processes may have influenced the dancing plague. It examines the role of media, rumors, and public discourse in shaping perceptions, emotions, and behaviors related to the phenomenon. It also discusses the impact of social amplification on the spread of the dancing plague beyond its initial epicenter. Furthermore, it reflects on the implications of the social amplification of risk for public health interventions and crisis communication.

Structural and cultural determinants play a significant role in shaping individual and collective behavior. This section explores the structural and cultural factors that contributed to the occurrence and persistence of the dancing plague. It examines the social, economic, and political conditions of 16th-century Europe that may have created a fertile ground for the phenomenon. It also discusses the influence of cultural values, religious beliefs, and power structures on the manifestation and interpretation of the dancing plague. Additionally, it reflects on the broader implications of structural and cultural determinants for understanding collective behavior in different historical and cultural contexts.

The psychological and sociological perspectives on the dancing plague of 1518 have broader implications for contemporary understanding of collective behavior and epidemic outbreaks. This section reflects on the relevance of these perspectives in the context of modern society. It discusses how insights gained from the dancing plague can inform our understanding of mass psychogenic illness, social contagion in the digital age, and the sociocultural factors that shape public health interventions. Furthermore, it emphasizes the importance of interdisciplinary approaches and the integration of psychological and sociological perspectives in studying and addressing collective phenomena.

Chapter Fourteen

This chapter explores the representation and impact of the dancing plague of 1518 in popular culture. From literature to art to media, the dancing plague has captured the imagination of artists and creators across various mediums. This chapter delves into the ways in which the dancing plague has been depicted, interpreted, and reimagined, examining its cultural significance and enduring legacy in popular culture.

Literature has been a medium through which the dancing plague has been retold and fictionalized. This section examines notable literary works that have incorporated the dancing plague as a central theme or backdrop. It explores the motivations of authors, the artistic liberties taken, and the symbolic meanings attached to the dancing plague in these literary representations. It also discusses the impact of these works on popular perception and understanding of the phenomenon.

The dancing plague has inspired artists throughout history to create visual representations that capture its essence and evoke emotions. This section explores notable artworks that depict the dancing plague, including paintings, sculptures, and other visual mediums. It examines the artistic techniques employed, the symbolic imagery utilized, and the interpretations conveyed through these representations. Additionally, it discusses the cultural and historical context in which these artworks were created and their lasting influence on the perception of the dancing plague.

The dancing plague has also found its way onto the silver screen and the stage. This section explores cinematic and theatrical adaptations that have portrayed the dancing plague in various ways. It examines how filmmakers and playwrights have interpreted and presented the phenomenon, the narrative choices made, and the visual and auditory elements employed to convey the intensity and impact of the dancing plague. It also discusses the reception of these adaptations and their contribution to the popular understanding of the dancing plague.

Music and dance are natural mediums through which to explore and express the essence of the dancing plague. This section explores musical compositions and choreographic interpretations inspired by the dancing plague. It examines how composers and choreographers have captured the frenzy, the rhythm, and the emotional intensity of the phenomenon. It discusses the genres, styles, and techniques used to evoke the spirit of the dancing plague and examines the reception and impact of these musical and dance interpretations.

The dancing plague has permeated popular culture in various ways beyond direct representations. This section explores the influence of the dancing plague on popular culture, including its references in contemporary music, literature, film, and other forms of media. It examines how the dancing plague has become a symbol or metaphor for other cultural phenomena, and how it continues to inspire artistic creations and cultural discourse. Additionally, it discusses the fascination with the dancing plague and its enduring appeal in contemporary popular culture.

The representation of the dancing plague in popular culture offers insights into the cultural and historical interpretations of the phenomenon. This section explores the different ways in which popular culture has portrayed and interpreted the dancing plague in relation to broader cultural and historical contexts. It examines the themes, motifs, and narratives that emerge in popular cultural depictions and reflects on the cultural meaning-making processes at play. Furthermore, it discusses how these interpretations contribute to the ongoing dialogue surrounding the dancing plague's significance in our collective consciousness.

The dancing plague has become a cultural symbol with multifaceted meanings and associations. This section explores the symbolic significance of the dancing plague in popular culture. It examines the metaphorical interpretations attached to the phenomenon, including themes of mass hysteria, societal constraints, collective liberation, and the power of transformative experiences. It delves into the ways in which the dancing plague has been used as a metaphor for societal and individual issues, such as conformity, rebellion, liberation, and the human capacity for irrational behavior. Additionally, it discusses the broader cultural and psychological implications of the dancing plague as a symbol and its resonance in contemporary society.

Popular culture is dynamic, constantly evolving and adapting to the changing times. This section explores how the representation and interpretation of the dancing plague have evolved over the years in popular culture. It examines the shifts in artistic styles, narrative approaches, and cultural contexts that have influenced the portrayal of the dancing plague in different eras. It also discusses the ways in which popular culture has adapted the dancing plague to reflect contemporary concerns, values, and artistic trends.

Popular culture plays a significant role in shaping public perception and understanding of historical events and phenomena. This section reflects on the impact of the dancing plague's portrayal in popular culture on how it is perceived and understood by the general public. It examines the ways in which popular cultural depictions have influenced public awareness, knowledge, and misconceptions about the dancing plague. Furthermore, it discusses the responsibility of artists, creators, and cultural influencers in accurately representing historical events while allowing for creative interpretation.

The portrayal of the dancing plague in popular culture also raises important questions about cultural appropriation and misrepresentation. This section explores instances where the dancing plague has been commodified or distorted for entertainment purposes, potentially disregarding the historical context and cultural significance of the phenomenon. It delves into the ethical considerations surrounding the representation of the dancing plague and emphasizes the importance of respectful and responsible engagement with historical events in popular culture.

The dancing plague has served as a wellspring of inspiration for artists, writers, and creators across generations. This section examines the ways in which the dancing plague has sparked creativity, imagination, and artistic innovation. It discusses how the phenomenon's inherent mystery, psychological intrigue, and historical significance have motivated artists to explore new artistic avenues and narratives. Additionally, it highlights the ongoing relevance and resonance of the dancing plague as a source of inspiration for contemporary artistic expressions.

Chapter Fifteen

Throughout this book, we have explored the intriguing phenomenon of the Dancing Plague of 1518. From its mysterious outbreak in Strasbourg to its spread across neighboring towns and regions, the dancing plague has captivated our curiosity and challenged our understanding of collective behavior. We have examined the various aspects surrounding this extraordinary event, including its historical context, the descriptions of the dance itself, the medical and religious explanations put forth, the theories and speculations offered by modern scholars, the social and cultural factors at play, the responses and interventions by authorities, the impact on daily life, and its historical significance and interpretations. We have also delved into the comparisons with other epidemics, the psychological and sociological perspectives, the representation of the dancing plague in popular culture, and the implications for contemporary understanding.

The dancing plague of 1518 remains a perplexing historical event that continues to intrigue researchers, scholars, and the public. While many questions still remain unanswered, our exploration has shed light on various aspects of the phenomenon. We have discovered that the dancing plague was not a solitary occurrence but rather part of a broader historical context of epidemic outbreaks and collective behavior. We have learned that medical and religious explanations, although prevalent at the time, were limited in their understanding and failed to fully account for the complexity of the dancing plague. We have examined the theories and speculations put forth by modern scholars, highlighting the multidisciplinary nature of the phenomenon and the need for a comprehensive approach to its study.

A central theme that emerged throughout our investigation was the significant role of social and cultural factors in the occurrence and persistence of the dancing plague. We have observed how societal beliefs, cultural practices, and the power dynamics of the time contributed to the collective response and interpretation of the phenomenon. The dancing plague was not merely a medical or psychological occurrence; it was deeply intertwined with the social fabric of 16th-century Europe. Our exploration of social and cultural factors has underscored the importance of considering the broader context in understanding collective behavior and its implications for public health interventions.

While the dancing plague of 1518 may seem distant and disconnected from our modern world, its study offers valuable lessons for contemporary understanding. The phenomenon provides insights into the complexities of collective behavior, the role of societal factors in shaping individual and group responses, and the interplay between psychological, sociological, and cultural dimensions. The psychological and sociological perspectives we have explored highlight the relevance of interdisciplinary approaches in unraveling the mysteries of collective behavior and epidemic outbreaks. The dancing plague serves as a reminder that historical events can offer valuable insights into our present-day challenges, enabling us to develop more effective strategies for addressing collective phenomena in our increasingly interconnected world.

The dancing plague of 1518 stands as a testament to the enduring nature of human behavior. While our world has transformed in many ways since the 16th century, fundamental aspects of human psychology and sociocultural dynamics remain constant. The dancing plague reminds us that we are susceptible to collective behavior, influenced by our social and cultural contexts, and driven by our emotions and beliefs. It serves as a reminder that understanding collective phenomena requires us to consider both individual experiences and societal factors, bridging the gap between psychology and sociology.

As we conclude our exploration of the dancing plague, we acknowledge that there is much more to uncover and understand. Many aspects of the phenomenon remain enigmatic, and new research and discoveries may shed further light on its causes, spread, and implications. We encourage further research to delve deeper into the factors that contributed to the dancing plague and to explore the phenomenon from additional perspectives. Interdisciplinary collaborations among historians, psychologists, sociologists, medical professionals, and cultural scholars can enhance our understanding of collective behavior and its implications for public health, social dynamics, and cultural phenomena.

Beyond its historical and scientific significance, the dancing plague of 1518 is ultimately a human story. It is a story of a community grappling with a bewildering and disruptive event, of individuals caught in the grip of an uncontrollable compulsion, and of the efforts made by authorities and practitioners to contain and understand the phenomenon. It is a story that reminds us of the complexities and mysteries of human behavior, the power of collective consciousness, and the resilience of communities in the face of adversity. The dancing plague serves as a reminder that history is not merely a collection of facts and events but a tapestry woven by the experiences, actions, and beliefs of individuals.

As we reflect on the dancing plague of 1518, we can draw several lessons that have relevance beyond the specific event. Firstly, it reminds us of the importance of open-mindedness and a willingness to explore unconventional explanations when faced with inexplicable phenomena. The dancing plague challenges our preconceived notions and forces us to consider the complex interplay of psychological, sociological, and cultural factors in shaping human behavior. Secondly, it highlights the need for interdisciplinary collaboration and holistic approaches in understanding and addressing collective phenomena. The dancing plague resists reductionist explanations, calling for a nuanced understanding that incorporates various perspectives and disciplines. Finally, it underscores the enduring power of historical events to captivate our imaginations and shape our cultural expressions. The dancing plague continues to resonate in popular culture, inspiring artistic works and provoking contemplation about the human condition.

The dancing plague of 1518 has left a legacy. It has intrigued scholars, inspired artists, and sparked curiosity for centuries. It challenges our understanding of collective behavior, shedding light on the intricate relationship between individual experiences and societal factors. The dancing plague serves as a reminder of the complexities of the human psyche, the power of cultural beliefs, and the ways in which historical events shape our present and future. Its legacy lives on as a fascinating chapter in the annals of human history, inviting us to continue exploring, questioning, and learning from the mysteries that surround us.

In conclusion, the dancing plague of 1518 remains a remarkable and enigmatic event that continues to captivate our collective imagination. Through a multidisciplinary exploration of its historical context, medical and religious explanations, social and cultural factors, and impact on daily life, we have gained valuable insights into this extraordinary phenomenon. It has demonstrated the interconnectedness of psychology, sociology, and culture in shaping collective behavior and has provided lessons for contemporary understanding. The dancing plague serves as a reminder that the complexities of human behavior transcend time, and its legacy invites us to delve deeper, ask further questions, and uncover new layers of understanding.

Printed in Great Britain
by Amazon

28576993R00059